Grim Honey

Grim Honey

Jessica Barksdale

Sheila-Na-Gig Editions

Volume 8

Author photo: © Rachel Breen
Cover art: iStock/SarapulSar38

ISBN: 978-1-7354002-1-1
Library of Congress Control Number: 2020946003

Published by Sheila-Na-Gig Editions
Russell, KY
Hayley Mitchell Haugen, Editor
www.sheilanagigblog.com

For Mitchell and Julien

Acknowledgments

Cathexis Northwest: "This Is It"

The Chacalaca Review: "Grim Honey"

Chiron Review: "What We Learn When We Learn Italian"

The Commuter: "You Over There, You"

Gyroscope: "Curve, Wave"

matchbook: "Knock, Knock"

The Missing Slate: "Frankenstein's Monster Goes to the Bathroom"

Negative Capability: "The Robin Does Not Know"

North American Review: "Unripped," "How Astonishing," "I Forget About Fame"

OVS Magazine: "Spoon Rest"

The Paddock Review: "New Episode of Jane the Virgin Now Available"

Rat's Ass Review: "Middle"

Ruminate: "Photograph, Late 1980s"

Sky Island Journal: "The World Was Once an Ocean"

Straight Forward Poetry: "Ocean Beach"

Tule Review: "Indiscrimination" and "Three Sisters"

West Trestle Review: "Courtship"

Honors

"Grim Honey" was a finalist in the Kallisto Gaia Julia Darling Memorial Poetry Prize 2019. "The Robin Does Not Know" was a finalist in *Negative Capability's* Spring 2020 poetry contest.

"How Astonishing" and "Unripped" were runners-up for *North American Review's* 2020 James Heart Prize in poetry. "I Forget About Fame" was a finalist. "Unripped" was a finalist in *The Sewanee Review's* 2019 poetry contest.

"Knock, Knock" also appeared in *Best Microfiction 2019* and was nominated by *The Wigleaf* as one of their Top 50 for 2019.

"Photograph, Late 1980s" was a finalist in New Millennium's 2020 contest.

"So We Could Fight" was shortlisted for *Cagibi Journal's* Macaron Prize.

"Unripped" was nominated by *North American Review* for a 2020 Pushcart Prize.

Contents

Unripped

You're the sixth of the seven almonds
Barack Obama ate every night his entire presidency.

You're the last breath before a blue
whale submerges, its Volkswagen-sized heart pulsing in the deep.

You're a wooden rowboat floating over the whale,
the fisherman with one oar. No, two.

You're the fax machine a year before we stopped using them,
the unsigned check from a large, accessible account,

the parking ticket unwritten in the officer's back pocket.
You're raw sugar piled in a china dish, a deck of fresh playing cards,

a sharpened, unused pencil. A pencil sharpener.
You're the credit card bill in its crisp envelope, unopened.

You're the untorn meniscus, the unchanged flight plan,
the apron pocket before it's ripped.

Everything hums. Your hopes, your un-canceled plans,
your dirt hidden under bookshelves and behind couches.

You're the uneaten baby wren, the raven the next tree over.
You're the wag of my dogs' tails before they poop;

you're the dementia circling my mother's present moment.
You're gold-framed, big eyed, three years old, staring,

daring me to let this moment pass. It never has,
not once, you the event un-shoehorned, you the ripe, sharp radish,

you in your overalls, baby Keds, red sweatshirt,
the foggy sky seconds from cracking into blue.

How Astonishing

Nuthatch, a pitchfork in my mouth.
Outdoors, saw, sawzall, chain saw, weed whacker, hell.

We call nuthatches Meeps because they *meep meep meep*
a sound brighter than the racket.

The air smells like possibility. Still morning. Hope.
You down there, the nuthatch calls. Fucking pay attention.

Meanwhile, *meep*. Polar bears swim to dry, savage land.
No snow, no prey. Pray.

Have you ever thought you were witnessing the final
conflagration? This the end-of-days, this the apocalypse?

Everyone has thought so. Only now, it might be true.
The sky sounds like airplanes.

One nuthatch minus one brown creeper equals a cypress
tree with a beetle infestation. *Meep*.

The world has fallen asleep.
Thank god. Maybe that's rain in the distance.

Today, there will be no wildfire.
How astonishing. The dirt, the plants, the array of insects.

A nuthatch breeds in old-growth woodlands. Sorry
about that deforestation thing.

We thought xenophobia was bad. Try astrophobia
as our spaceships launch, we leaving it all behind,

the wet and silted, the ragged and ruined,
the broken and betrayed. *Meep*.

The Robin Does Not Know

Inside the darkened house, the pandemic
is our unwelcome, slick guest, gobbling

up the internet, time, and conversation.
We can't shut him up, this viral king,

this apocalypse harbinger we've nurtured
in verse and song, this pale-horsed terror,

this Kali Yuga, this Ragnarok, this end-of-times poster prince.
He slides into bed between us, whispering all night

about toilet paper and our children who live faraway.
So sad, he murmurs. *Tragic.*

He chuckles over the grandchild
we can see only through sent photos,

our parents who are on lockdown, their frail, papery
bodies defenseless against the king's sharp

claws. *Move over*, he says, nestling close, wrapping
arms around us both. *Breathe me in.*

He snores loud and long, a sinus
drumbeat of *die, die, die.* In the wee hours,

we sneak out of bed, huddle together near the fire,
plot grocery runs, plan doctor calls, evaluate milk and bread stores.

Meanwhile, outside, the sun comes up, predictable
as the king but more frequent. The frogs croak

awake, the Canada geese honk, the robin perches atop
the blossoming plum and sings over and over and over

It is almost spring. It will be spring, and then it will be summer.
The king will leave our bed, clinging to the ratty edge
of a garage couch, unlistened to.
Go, we whisper, *now.*

Grim Honey

I try to break up, be done already,
but memories twist inside me,
mismanaged, yanking hard.

Break an irreverent verb:
To hold with slivered palms.
They may have died,

bodies disgorging potent juices,
their last days bruises
on the permanent record,

but they're still here,
poisonous, delicious
sugar cubes of story,

moths to the lemon,
slippery wax on the floor
I always walk on.

I may hate them,
but I love a few like a hammer,
something I can smash

regularly, sorrow
a nail, ache a door
desperate to be demolished,

melancholy a hopeless meteor
I miss, image blurry
in the telescope.

Once my dead sister asked,
"Did Halley's comet ever land?"
We laughed so hard

we peed ourselves.
She's the comet flinging
toward us, steady

as a ring, around and around.
She's the grim honey
from last year's harvest,

a sweet, ambered fossil,
slicing my tongue
with each sharp lick.

Cold Enough to Break Bones

December is cold enough to break bones,
so I don't need the extra whack of wet wood, shin cracking

against railroad ties and gravel. I don't need
to cry on the frozen ground, whimpering for my husband

like I used to for my mother. He was there to pull me up
off the ground and limp-step me up the stairs.

Everyone in my family born in December is dead,
my father, my sister, my grandmother, all slipped back into the eternal.

Today, I prepare for their birthdays, nurse my swollen shin and
ankle with water stiff and cold enough to slice my body open

and spill the frozen sadness to the ground, drip like water
from the very ice I place against my tingling skin.

I lift the dripping bag of cubes and turn my ankle. My skin shivers
and clacks with nerves and blood, everything, all at once, coming to the surface.

Ocean Beach

– From the photograph, *Ocean Beach, SF, 1976*

When these girls
jetéd over the beach,
ballet arms before them,
water just under
their pointed toes,
my father was still alive.

I press toward the photograph,
my nose against glass,
breathing misty forty-three-year-old salt.
If I watch long enough,
I will see the dancers touch down
and twirl into the crystal waves.

I search past the girls' flying forms,
past the heavy man in plaid shirt,
past the children in the surf
dipping cupped palms into foam.

Out to the horizon, nothing
but black and white sky.
On the beach, people
who may still be alive,
women who may still be dancing,
children who have grown up to have
children of their own.

I am not on this beach, but I could have been,
my arms once as limber as the girls'.
I could go right now, drive to the edge
of the continent,
open the door to the air
of this photograph,
but the girls
are long gone,
and so is my father.

My Mother Read

My mother read through my father's
absence, consuming mysteries in bed
when we went back to school,
histories during afternoon
homework, romances at night
after Hamburger Helper.

She showered and dressed, dusted
the living room furniture, vacuumed
deep lines into the red carpet, folded
lunches into brown paper bags,
but she called us Elmore and Roosevelt
and Tatiana instead of who we thought
we were, who we used to be
before our father withered and shrunk
into his disease, so thin at the last,
we imagined his cancer
circling his stomach like snakes.

Then, one year, long after one sister developed
diabetes and refused to cooperate
with doctors, hiding first Snickers
and then Smirnoff under her pillow,
and another threw up her dinner
into a Tupperware bowl she kept under her bed,
and another gained and lost so much weight
she had three sizes of pants in her closet,
our mother put down her books
and turned to us, her children, one now dead,
one moved across the country, one resentful
of having had to watch it all.

Our mother looked at us and said,
"What happened?"

Three Sisters
– after Sylvia Plath

We were three speckled roses,
oranges in the fruit trees, gardens
with tears, sugars kneeling at winter.

Point is, we were growing, frocks
flouncing, Easter queens, daughters
to our father, rain in the distance.

Time dripped itself loose, and we were still three
but now at war, our feelings bridegrooms
attached to other lovers. Feral, stone,

we the black under, tasting what we could
when we could and in secret.
This the broken bower, growing

in its ugliness, we three flung away as if by sharp
antlers, our home peeling, powdery, gone.
It's too late. One dead. One burrowed

in another country. Me here writing.
But I still see us, triangle touching, we under
the branches, reaching out, light-green tendrils,

warm, round, musky with afternoon.

Hand-Painted

My father died in August
and left us half a pink house,
a half-shingled playhouse,
a half-remodeled downstairs.
He would start one project
and move to the next,
never imagining
he'd die before
completing any.

The next summer,
I rode my bike to the hardware store
and ordered for delivery eight gallons
of brown paint and every brush
and roller the clerk recommended.
Before I started, I did nothing
I should have. No scraping or priming.
No inspections for rot
or missing nails or ripped
window screens.

Instead, I banged the ladder
against the first pink wall
and smashed/slathered the brown
over what he didn't do.
My messy brush met
the unfinished rows of shingle
and clapboard. I didn't worry
the margins.
How could you, I muttered
with each stroke, every day,
until the house was covered,
one rough color,
my hands and arms
dark and oily from sun
and chemicals.
How could you?

Photograph Late 1980s

We lived into the decay: the wooden retaining wall
buckling, the fence leaning back in reverse swan dive,
the concrete patio my father and the neighbors
poured sporting tufts of dandelions and Johnson grass.

Behind us, the barn-style tool shed where forgotten things
moldered: my grandmother's steamer trunk, our childhood
toys, broken furniture. It hulks behind the untended flowerbeds
and the weedy green upper tier. In the dark depths of the yard,

a bower of walnut trees, where thankfully, I can see nothing.
A woman I don't remember sits on the far side of the ancient
picnic table drinking water from a tall glass. One man, now dead,
sits opposite her and looks into the camera, the only one who does.

Sturdy, solid, he's the captain of this party with his boat shoes, pipe,
white beard. Next to him in a metal outdoor rocker, my youngest
sister. Next to her, my husband, though I can only see one brown leg,
one gleaming white sock, one immaculate tennis shoe. Those legs.

My sister's right leg is also on display, darkened, wrong, shiny strips
of flesh on her shin, thigh, burns from an electric shaver,
she oblivious as she pressed too hard into her own skin, destroying
hair and the top layer of her body for beauty. *Neuropathy,*

the doctors said, but by then, she was in the hospital awaiting skin
graft surgery, the first of which failed, the second leaving her
with scars I see from thirty years away. But now she's talking
with my husband, drinking a diet soda, bottle-blonded back

to the hair color she was born with, that white-haired baby
come home five days old, red and squalling. That baby I cradled
here on this patio, my father holding the camera. That baby
the ghost in this photo, that baby and my father. Me, too,

because I'm off stage, in the kitchen with my mother, hiding
from my uncle's relentless party lens, but really, ducking
from these truths: The backyard will collapse, my marriage
will fail, my sister will die.
We have four years. Maybe five.

Let's Take a Walk

and talk about candy.
Your favorite? *KitKat*.
Me? though I have given up
sweets for the sake of my thighs,
Tootsie Pop.
You move slow, attached to tubes,
bags, a rolling pole.
Me? Wide smile
not matching my mood, a tumble
of ghouls.

Let's talk about candy.
Necco Wafers, Three Musketeers, Snickers.
Oh, the falsity of that bar, peanuts
a sly promise of health.
Your son likes *Starburst*; his girlfriend, *Mounds*.
Our mutual friend, *York Peppermint Patty*.
Oh! Grinning plastic pumpkin heads on every nursing station.
Reach in, grab.

Let's take a walk
and talk about candy. Good old
Hershey's, Payday, Good & Plenty.
We know what we like by now.
Twenty years of cancer. Now this,
a stroll in the hospital hallways.
Maybe a song as we contemplate
Rocky Road, Pez, and *Mars Bars*.

Candy, a tingle,
a spark, a swirl of sugar,
and then not.

You Were the Tender

If there had been a harpsicord tucked in a cozy corner,
you would have played it from memory,

a pull of fingers toward mastery.
Innate, intrinsic, as if you grew up in Prague

to wealthy, educated parents in another century,
swamped with attention, you a brilliant

phlox, tended in the family's conservatory
with the azaleas (they would have been smart, too).

If you'd grown up in a five-star hotel,
the adjoining room would have been filled

with mad scientists, sitting still and open as mollusks,
experimenting with quantum entanglement theorems that, yes,

you'd have understood. You would have gently handed
over your diary as a gift, providing them the formula

for the question that worried them the most.
They would have clapped your back and presented

brandy, a cigar, admittance to a club none of us could join.
While sitting at a campfire on a wind-banged archipelago,

you would have charted the speed of the approaching
hurricane and thwarted it. You would have constructed a gilt

skylight for your tent to observe winter bird migration and wind shear.
You would have crafted a method for digging through slate

to provide us with indoor plumbing, we holding our fractured bones,
hands injured claws after trying to save ourselves from ourselves.

At night, you'd do the gourmet cooking with a bent tin fork
and a cast-iron pan, toasted coriander and sautéed onions filling the air,

the meal presented on a plank table you'd earlier hewn from driftwood,
the night lit by homemade candles, wicks hissing seaweed.

You had the key to the worst padlock. You were the ship
unperturbed by the towering iceberg. You were the tender blue

sound of every tune that whistled through your head like stars,
the glimmering reds and shy pinks of your hundreds of nail polishes,

the sweet waft of your passion fruit perfume in the dark hallways.
This was you when you were here.

Yahrtzeit

For hours, I gripped her body to mine
as she moaned and shat, moaned and shat.

Her daughter piped morphine into her mouth
as we waited for the hospice nurse,

who didn't come, didn't come, didn't come,
nor did peace. Finally, a relative,

my relief—not my friend's—arrived,
and I left, exhausted, numb, shocked

by the pain, the smells, the grief, sliding back
into my life, maybe watching TV,

only to awaken to a call from one friend
to tell me our beloved was dead, and then later,

from another who phoned to apologize
that they hadn't let me see her body

before she was driven away by hearse.
A year later, to the hour, I write, angry,

desperate to see her at the rest
she worked so hard for.

I traveled with her through that labor
and saw no result from the struggle,

and even though a year has passed,
I can't find my quiet, dead friend.

Yet at every turn, I'm still holding her.
I can't let go.

Lull

On your elbow, propped.
A mild summer day, brie, a baguette,
a bottle of sparkling cider.
Somewhere, children
not yours.
If you squint, a unicorn
hiding in the copse,
glinting, brilliant.

Adamantine, he says,
either a rock or an adjective,
you don't know. Maybe a number
on the periodic table,
an element hitherto unknown.

This is a calm you don't understand,
a moment before the inciting
incident, the countdown before Chernobyl,
the morning hours
before the bombs.
You lean back on the canvas pillow,
close your eyes,
wake up.

Condemnation

Welcome to this punishment, meted out just for you,
our special treat, tailored for your every transgression.
Something we arrived at without your consent or approval.

Here, walk through this metal gate. Ignore the slam. The heavy lock.
The key. Here, take a hard seat. Watch those manacles,
shackles. Sit back to the wall, eye on the door.

There. Better now? You knew this was coming.
You've been waiting your whole life, looking over your shoulder
for this ugly shoe to drop. Surprise! Here we are, *chez nous.*

Don't mind your cellmate. Just a little friend for the rest
of your life, however long that is. We'll figure it out. No,
he doesn't say much. Don't look at him in the eye. What did I tell you!

It is noisy. Sorry. No air-conditioning either. Why are we leaving?
You think we'll stay here with you? You petty liar, you cheat, you shirker.
This belongs to you, alone, the price you'll pay for all that you've done,

and we know what that is. We've been there all along. Watch us now
as we throw away the key, just as your mother said someone would.
You never really believed her. You thought you were special. You really did.

This is It

I will not attempt a reformation
of your ornate theology

but tell you of mine, which is none,
at least on my sane days.

On others, I believe we are all
spits of energy repeatedly

birthed to practice life
on this planet, trying

out bodies like new clothing,
the ultimate vacation,

self-help retreat,
meditation practice.

I spent years as an animal,
mostly dog and cat.

Though my fear of death suggests
many quick insect lives. Whap!

We don't progress to human
but bound like pool balls

across the green velvet
of experience. Coyote, mantis,

chimp, human, black bear, giant squid.
At some point, we don't come back,

figuring something out,
whatever it may be.

This is what I believe
when I don't believe

we are here,
and then we are not.

New Episode of Jane the Virgin Available

One

Mary was not the first.
Chimalma swallowed the stone
that became Quetzalcoatl.
Maya's elephant dream
turned into the Buddha.
One virgin after the other, episode
upon episode of divine pregnancy,
amazing birth to a god-like child,
the mother disappearing or dying
or sitting back in wonder.
My son. Would you just look at him!
My work here is done.
And here we are, season two,
Jane clinging to her virginity plot point,
a lifeline to television immortality
and financial gain.
Whatever you do,
don't write a penis into that scene.

Two

I had no takers until one night before high school graduation.
There he was, at the party for the whole school,
someone I didn't know because otherwise, no dice.
Gold in his brown hair, shirt open at the neck,
pucca necklace. Or something silver. Coke spoon.
Angel flight pants. Or jeans.
The long vinyl bench seat of my mother's station wagon,
nothing going well, me like a clenched rock, too tight
for this magic to pass through.
But this boy plugged away, and I was swimming,
moving, floating on the seat, bleeding, bleeding, all that blood
from a tiny piece of skin that means so much to countless viewers.
He left, and I sat there, clutching the steering wheel,
looking out into the hazy mooned night,

even though there was nothing to wait for.
My potential miracles ripped open and thrashed in bloody streaks.
Nothing but the rest of my life, and now one less thing to give up.
One step closer to nothing.

Three

Yes to the slash of vinyl gore,
and yes to the moon, round and white
on the car's hood. Yes to the humped
and botched thing that is living,
this crawling beast of mud, looking to heaven.

Boxed

On a walk in the dead of winter,
I found a box, cardboard tossed
from a now-gone car.
A graduation photo. Report cards:
Larry is a wonderful student.
A small Santa bell that wobbled out a tune.
Diplomas, birthday cards, scattered photos.

I was tempted to take the Santa,
but instead, I tidied the box
and put it on the curb, hoping Larry would
jerk his car to a stop and gather it home.

A mile later, another box, this one labeled: *Larry's Funeral.*
Inside, the guestbook of all who attended:
Ann Sunderland. Marvin Hinkshaw, Gina Smith.
Larry would not be coming to collect
his belongings. A quick story follows

about how I reunited Larry's things with his sister
through the neighborhood list serve and Google maps.
Thieves had picked the wrong boxes to steal
from her garage. *I wanted his son to have his things,*
she wrote me. *No one else could use them.*
No one could. Still, I think about what Larry left,
how unconnected I was to each object,
how unfamiliar every item in his boxes. How known.

Curve, Wave

I was never built of edges but curves and waves, nothing clean
about my fleshy form, but I lived anyway, pummeling forward.

Fat my history, no knobby spine, gangly knee, pointy elbow.
My sisters built of corners and angles, sharp of jaw, strong of line,

me cobbled of ancient, sturdy DNA scrapped from creatures
still scared of dinosaurs, haunted by ice and magma, built to survive

the earth's tumult. Back then, women needed flesh. Wobbly bellies.
Fatty layers. Jiggly juices. Otherwise, they stayed empty, barren.

Sex was survival for the messy tribe. Glop, my caveman, protected
me from roar and venomous bite. Sure, I had a mind, but to exist,

I needed his hairy body and stone club. My genetic foremother
danced around a crackling fire without shame. Mirrors hadn't been

invented yet. She thrived in the garden, a golden age, when the good
glow came from the inside. Happiness from the sun and being alive

in the first place. Too bad I need this literary device, this flashback
backstory to feel okay about my arms, my chin. My feelings live

in different households. The older smarter feeling loves that I am alive.
My unhinged self still thinks I could look like Christie Brinkley

if I only tried. Overhead, the full white moon, huge, drifting in her
enormous way. Nothing in space gives one shit she's round, white,

and pock-marked. She beams. I reveal myself, craving her safe shine.

Birthing Back

Bloody sheets,
bloody beds, bloody
clothing, bloody chairs,
nothing staunching that early
menstrual flow.
Blood clots the size
of fists, blood about babies,
the leading up to one,
or the letting go.

Parts that once worked,
no longer cooperated. Standing
made me bleed. Living, too.
So I had them yanked
and missed the bleeding,
the way it told me
who and when I was,
why I was angry, sad.
Why I spontaneously
harangued
others.

Now, babies grown
and gone, the life force
inside me weaker, feeble,
I sometimes dream of myself
in a bloody field. Not war. Not death.
Not indiscriminate slaughter.
But me, a body atop
the red slick of myself,
slipping, sliding, pushing
forward, birthing
myself back.

Middle

Skin, brain, organs, those that remain,
that reproductive flap long ago heaped into medical waste.
Teeth, eyes, stomach, that last foul,
caustic beast always prickly.
Nervous as a child,
pangy cramps gripping
with sharp claws as the school bus blasted by,
she straining on the only toilet,
her sister pounding on the door.
Who needed Monday morning spelling tests,
teasing, socks slipping as she ran on the playground,
hair wet from morning fog?
Her underwear, of course, baggy.
Shoes tight at big toes, hair a crooked, kitchen-chair cut,
dress hems gaping mouths where she caught them on her bike seat,
riding illegally in the afternoons before changing into play clothes.

All of that a half century ago,
where time lives, in her fingers, on the screen,
all the hours in the wrong classrooms, dust
in linoleum corners,
teachers with clacking high-heeled shoes,
the afternoons hot and long and smelly, ripe
with the slow girl in the back row who peed
in widening yellow puddles.
The smack of bombardment balls against ribs,
the cold of rainy day asphalt rasping her knees.
But she could chase and skip and swing for hours,
a whirl on the bars, round and round and round.

What once zipped and hummed inside her is dying,
but what didn't work is finally kicking in.
Like not caring about shoes or hems or hair, walking
into the store a wild, just awakened wreck but smiling
at the cashier anyway.
You don't like her?
Go fuck yourself, and she means it.

Do, though, kindly pass the flaxseed, hemp hearts,
cranberry supplement, probiotic,
ground-up cow cartilage because her limber
low-down is gone, joints aching,
bone-on-bone, a gasping step one and step two.
Achilles, ah! Knees, oh!
Hand her the stronger reading glasses.
The vaginal hormone suppositories. The melatonin.
Maybe an ear horn. (What did you say?)
A diaper, a pot brownie, a window with a view.
Who are you, anyway?
She thinks she likes you.
She's sure you didn't mean any of it.

Birth Day

My friend lay supine on the planet, a meteor shower
draped in front of her lest she glimpse

her own atmosphere. Floating above, I witnessed
the climate change, two doctors wrestling

her wildfire abdomen. In a ticking clock of black holes and comets,
I beheld the kingfisher rip-tide flurry. *Don't watch,*

her mother whispered, her voice a prairie of fear
as she gripped her daughter's hand. I couldn't stop.

The slice, the tsunami tumbling in, whoosh,
jellyfish, night squid, sea monster. And then,

a whole universe plopped on my friend's belly.
Another slice, peeling open the red pulsing orb

to wrest a baby out of the undergrowth.
Today, that baby is fifteen, currently an otter slug

erosion wilderness rainforest swamp. We pray
honeybee forget-me-not sugarcane

peace rose will come, in due time.
Alive because of her mother's solar rotations,

the spinning and churn of spheres and stars, life
cracking open, spewing her forth, wailing, bloody, whole.

Frankenstein's Monster Goes to the Bathroom

In the dead dark of a moonless night,
in a cemetery strewn with Spanish moss,
the mad scientist fossicked amongst rejected limbs
and ancient bones, digging up a torn rotator cuff,
an irritable bowel, age-spotted,
potentially pre-cancerous skin,
two Achilles tendons stretched like taffy.

His prize find? A lump of brain dulled
and fogged, no memory, no recall,
the stream of thought a constant
"Those thingies" and "Whatevers."

Lightening flashed, Igor stumbled past clutching his hump.
With a jolt, I was transformed from one thing into another,
what was once firm was now loose and flabby,
what was once alert now hazy, half blind,
mostly wrecked, a total mess.

Before bed, I was a woman in her late forties,
but part by part, I was replaced with the used and tired.
the bungled and the botched,
the crazed man racing around my body,
affixing me with wires and tubes, screaming,
"It's alive! My god! It's alive!"

Later, after everything, I wobbled out of bed,
grabbing a wall, a dresser.
I tripped over my actual two left feet,
lurched toward the bathroom, arms outstretched,
a round moan in my wide open mouth.
I was a woman unable to navigate her own house,
everything unclear, difficult,
the toilet there,
no there.
No there.

Courtship

Long before the big box stores and strip malls,
miles of rich alluvial farmland,
plant rows all the way to the horizon.
On Sunday afternoons, we pedaled the flat
and forever roads,
the air dust and grain and chemicals.
Asphalt ripping hot under our bike tires,
a *whisk whisk, whisk whisk.*
You looking for peaches and sweet corn to pick.
Me in a skirt and sandals,
your calves brown and strong,
your head turning to tell me something,
laughing as we rode away from our college town.
But then the white farmhouse,
the picket fence, the open gate.
There, the goose with its sharp yellow bill,
fat with huge webbed feet, bigger than any English holiday dinner.
"Gear up," you'd tell me, both of us pumping hard, my hem flapping.
Harder and harder, faster and faster.
The goose, neck thrust out, bill pointed, propelled
itself like a torpedo down the farmhouse path,
honking and honking and honking.
It pecked our legs, knees, feet,
as if warning us to stay away, never come back,
to stop all of it.
If only we'd paid attention.

Quake

When we first toured the house,
we opened a small door at the back
of the garage and stepped through
into the gloom, filtered yellow
light slatting sideways from the vents.

We stared up at the insulation
someone installed backward
and the foundation that triangled
and jagged up the California hill,
the clay soil breaking into clods

under our shoes, the air full of dust
and the tinge of rat droppings.
After we bought the house
and carted in our children
and worldly possessions,

retrofitters strapped and bolted
the house to the concrete,
reinforcing the walls with extra boards
and thick slabs of plywood.
A decade before in another house,

we'd lived through the Loma Prieta
earthquake and understood the importance
of holding things tight, but this time,
we forgot to strap me down.
It only took five years to shake me loose.

Spoon Rest

At night, we slept like moving spoons,
fitting one way
and then the other in the drawer
of our married bed.

Even when we fought,
even when I was going to leave,
at night, the warmth of your arm
around me, the press
of our knees and thighs and chests.

When I walked into the house
after so many years,
carrying our son's
bags, thumping them
down in the empty
kitchen, I saw the spoon
rest, the one I bought
twenty-five years ago
for an apartment
we could not find.

One child, another on the way,
we lived in my mother's house,
sleeping in my childhood
bed, our son in a crib
in the same room.
On sale, a ceramic spoon rest,
blue and white, an etched chicken
in the wide dip,
ready to catch what I spilled.
I stored it in the closet,
finally unpacking it when we found
the apartment, carrying
it with me to each new house.

In the rush of trying
to pull away, I forgot to pack it up,
and there it was, on the counter
next to the tea kettle,
just where I left it.

Ending

– after the painting *Le Rue Annette* by Sir David Young Cameron

Walking in the Marais
or Montmartre, some *arrondissement* with small
streets and the shadows
of stuccoed buildings
with crooked wooden shutters.
It is always summer,
both of us sightseeing and sweaty,
dust in the creases
of our necks, on our shoes, in our mouths,
you and I alone now, confused
without children, traveling in Europe
in hopes that our future would come true—
college sweethearts forever in love
not a myth.

I fumble for words, blurt out Spanish
instead of French, your Spanish much better
but equally useless.
We stumble into cafés and bars,
sit, use our eight best words:
Deux cafés crème et deux pains au chocolat,
hoping to be understood,
by them, each other,
our unhappiness a still life
of beige and light browns,
maybe a burst of russet
as the shadows creep across the street,
day turning to night even as the blue sky beckons.
We sip and stare at customers
rushing into the *epicerie.*

Before leaving, we unwrap the dark chocolates,
one on each saucer, place
the slim rectangles on our tongues,
find nothing sweet.

It Goes Without Saying

When reading a map,
a syllabus,
or a prescription bottle,
start at the beginning
and don't skip
the crucial information
that will lead you to the main highway,
the right assignment,
the correct dose,
the exact information
that will save your life.

Also, while you're at it,
think about leaving home
five minutes earlier
to avoid being five minutes late.
It's a math problem
that always works,
a truth that can't be avoided,
even when you wish it could.

And there are those tasks
you've put off for a millennium,
the unpacked boxes in the garage
from two moves ago,
the various sizes
of clothing at the back
of the spare-bedroom closet,
the hump of storm mud blocking
the shed door.
Worse things, of course,
like leaving a marriage or a job,
cutting off that dangerous love affair,
saying no to the best-loved child.
No matter the stuff,
not doing it
never gets it done.

Stacked one on top the other,
the little things become
the big things,
become your tagline,
your *nom de plume,* your
mantra, your slogan,
your signature dish.

Decide, is what I'm saying.

What We Learn When We Learn Italian

She is, and she has, and what flows
like wine is wine. And beer.
Sometimes milk, sometimes water,
one glass or two at dinner,
which is what she eats with uncles, nieces, and grandparents,
mostly because *to eat dinner* is its own verb.

He will ask her if she wants to eat dinner at nine.
We are in Italy, after all.
She will say *No, not nine. Ten,* refusing him
until time has cracked into the next day.
He asks about coffee, dessert, *digestivo,*
finally getting the message when she points
to his wife, *there.* And her husband, *here.*
Sometimes, in alarming chapters,
he asks her for a little kiss.
He tells her she's *molto carina.*
Again, she nods toward the town square
and her husband Mario standing by, near, next
to the church door.
Stop, she says. *Basta.*

Finally she goes off with Mario
who tells her she can buy one hat.
Only one, and nothing *troppo caro.*
After that, it's only a matter of hours, days, weeks,
months, and years until she hops on the train, plane, motor scooter
and visits Roma, Milano, Napoli, and Firenze.
She understands the rules of the table and the ordering
of *primi, secundi,* and *dolce.* If needed, she could toss
away her notes and set the table.
Snap, there's the tip on the checkered tablecloth.

Late in the book, she was finally in the past tense, having lived
through seasons and various weather, arriving
at her own apartment in a small hilltop village.
No one asked her to drink anything.

No one counted out money or cared
what time it was, not anymore.
Outside, the moon slid
the way it always had through
a sky finally hers.

You Over There, You

There you were on my ancient doorstep, late, or early, unannounced, in the thick black coat I bought you for Christmas. Of course, you were on your way, but when would you arrive?

As always, no phone. Me, no extra-key or place to hide it, only two days into my teaching abroad, Florence sodden, dark, full of shadows and confusion. But you convinced the smoking

college students on the cobblestone street—who knew me as professor mom—to let you through the first two doors, and then you were at mine, a one, two knock. Bearded, cold, smiling.

It was February, and you'd landed at Heathrow, taken a bus to the City of London airport. Then the flight and travel path went something like Frankfurt to Skopje.

Macedonia! You huddled on a frozen hill in the coat and in a down sleeping bag. Then to a rickety communist era train to Thessaloniki and on to Athens. Next a port town

I can't remember, maybe Patras, and a night ferry to Ancona and another train to Bologna and back to Florence until you found my building with directions jotted on a ragged

scrap of ferry napkin. Long ago, you and I were alone together in the small house, your father student teaching in another town, coming home on weekends. It was you

and me, day after day, me too young to mother properly, me in charge of you, already smarter and with a wicked baby smile. But there we were in the dark mornings,

the slog of the day. We went to every free Wednesday at the merry-go-round, every park. You and me together in the nighttime with fevers. Here, in Florence, in the medieval building, in the odd apartment, you and me once again, planning meals of roasted eggplant and *brocolo romanesco*, walking to the store pulling the cart behind us. You and me in Pisa, Lucca, Rome,

and Naples. The ferry trip to Procida, the walk across the island to eat at the restaurant where *Il Postino* was filmed. Then the journey around and back to the dock, the man who opened the bag

of oranges and beckoned us to take one, two, more, both of us eating while we strolled to the boats. Wandering Florence's churches, the nunnery, that half hour of echoing song.

The Zeffirelli Museum, no other patrons on that rainy afternoon, we two sitting in Dante's *Inferno*, an animated show drawn by the director. Hell was wild with color, fluid, beautiful.

The Uffizi, Boboli Gardens, finally getting you a phone. One Sunday morning walking up the hill to Fiesole, each of us eating a whole pizza at the bar at the crossroads. Walks before bed

to get the water from the *Piazza della Signoria* spigots, fresh and con gas, talking about free will and metaphors. You are a man now, not a baby, grey in your hair, a man caught up in his life.

Italy could never happen again, me free for months, without husband, you free, always, throwing off rules, our expectations, searching only for love. Late in the trip, that day in April, when you

brought your newly beloved to the apartment, we three hiking to the *Piazzale Michelangelo*, you both looking out toward the city, your arm around her thin shoulders, me behind

you now, taking the shot. Me still behind you, remembering, holding onto this precious cup of time, you, as you've always been, so unique, so impossible, so wonderful, you and me

over there, you and me over, you over there, you.

Shift

She thought a portmanteau
was a suitcase, a word
holding two things
instead of one.

She thought pulling anyone's plug
was out of the question
until her mother got old,
her life toppled and lurchy
and full of struggle.
If only, she thought, she could, feeling
the plastic plug dig into her palm,
the yank from the wall,
the silencing of monitors and machines.

She thought growing gray
was lazy, until she
got old. And gray, and
it was discovered dye
is toxic, a skullcap of carcinogenic
substances, spread monthly.
Now she looks in the mirror,
startled. Me?

Thus the world cracks the axis
of belief systems,
everything from eating meat—
a big no—
and drinking—never
again. Thus
what made sense
no longer does,
a live mother,
blonde hair,
a margarita at sunset,
all is pain,
and what was painful

is right.
Now, she stares into the winter
sky and seeks the
answers that will
come, or not.
In a month, the questions
may evaporate
like steam,
smoke, a flash,
over-night freeze.

Older Woman with Dogs

For weeks, you watch the gerbera daisies,
two lush plants with blooms clutching all the pinks

in every petal: fuscia, rose, coral, strawberry, almost red
near the yellow eye. In the mornings, the flowers are closed,

but in the afternoons, eyes wide open,
bubblegum tips arcing toward ground.

You try to ignore the blooms' companions, the spent crones
crumbling toward death while the youngsters waggle in the breeze.

Old stems loop over to support the crunchy brown nubs.
Easy to miss when right next to the cemetery, the nursery.

One day, an oddity: A flower off kilter, missing petals,
flower like a child's smile, full of tooth-shaped spaces.

But in the center of the eye, petals, inappropriate, misplaced,
a jagged V of pinks in the dead sunny middle.

You stop, your dogs circling for smells at your feet.
You take a photo, something for the Guinness Book

or a coffee table photo spread of natural mistakes.
Part of you wants to pick the flower,

to bring home proof that nature supports the different,
you, so like this flower, your petals in the wrong places,

some of your vitals missing, gaps exposed,
you a pink flower with a yellow eye mistake,

your wrong petals proving you are going off,
and won't leave, you, older woman with dogs, you older woman

with your strange petal placement, refusing
to join the dead husks yet, living, and living on.

Recalculating

In the car
it's easy,
directions
revised
and rewritten
without regrets
or recrimination,
the map realigned,
reconfigured,
the path clear,
everyone calm.

No emergency, just
a simple
recalculation.
No need to retrace
or reconnoiter,
the way obvious,
the next right
on a clearly marked street
a given.

So We Could Fight

We fought over whose dog was smarter and prettier,
which mutt had the smoothest fur or largest eyes.

Afterward, we slid silent into the cellar to taste the dog
kibble, crunchy and corny, like brothy breakfast cereal.

We fought about our younger siblings, arguing
who was cutest, then we tortured those we'd fought over

with taunts and sneaky pinches, running from our mothers'
yells, plunging down the street, around the corner, past

the house with the fierce black shepherd named Midnight,
past the pyracantha berry bush with its witchy fingers.

Later, we snuck back to my house, which had better
snacks. We fought about our hair (short was better. No long),

our rooms, our grades. You were invited to special dinners
and school clubs,waiting for me to fight back. From my chair

in the principal's office, I had no ammo. We fought about
who could share our time, new friends stealing one of us

away for days, sometimes years. But we always came back,
fighting over clothes and boys, who had to drive to the movies,

the mall, the beach, over tight synthetic floral tops and college
classes, until that last fight about your wedding and who

would be your maid of honor, me with two small children,
your other friend with nothing but time, so I shook you off,

let loose the strands of all our fights, forgetting you,
how your eyes glinted as you opened your front door

and let me inside so we could fight.

You Always Love the Broken Ones

The shy, the friendless, the hurt at home; the too short, tall, thin, and fat pull you into playground corners. Huddling between classroom buildings, you make up stories about ruling the world.

The ones who read tales of ancient, made up worlds rife with wizards and fairies and dark magic. Those who study for spelling tests.

Those with runny noses and sores on their scalps and awkward, damaged eyeglasses. Those who wear hearing aids and play with rubber trolls with aqua-colored hair. The ones who have to go to the office before lunch to take special pills.

Those bursting through puberty in scary breast blooms, grease, and hair. Those who hide in the bathrooms with gushing periods. Those who cry inappropriately.

The ones who talk too much or not at all. Those with deeply buried talents they will never find, or do, and when they grow up, they never return home.

The hair-puller, anorexic, bulimic, anxious, agoraphobic.

Boys who wish they were with boys—men who wish they were with men—but are with you instead.

Unannounced lesbians. Nerds. Comedians. Men who twitch or breathe through deviated septums.

Everyone of color in a time when color isn't bright. Foreign-exchange students.

Adjunct everyone. Spinsters, even though the word is out-of-date. Nihilists, anarchists, thieves.

Those with tight pants, ragged shoes, messy hair. The too smart or not smart enough.

You want them all, the dripping, staggering mess, the wretched, the wrecked, your shores awash, empty, waiting.

Fledglings

Raven chicks are the size of their parents,
needy, noisy giants hopping
from roof to branch to rail,
demented, screaming
to be fed.

Waa! they cry. *Waa!*
Grow up, I want to yell, staring
up at the bird family darkly
decorating an elm branch.
Then I relent.

Poor parents, nagged
to death by big babies.

When I was a baby, I patted
my mother's back
when she patted me.
At sixteen, my father dead,
I ran the house, driving
my sisters to events
and ordering around contractors.
Two years later, I moved out,
and my mother didn't call for a month.

Waa! I cried from my house five miles
away, but she didn't answer,
lost somewhere back in time,
most likely her childhood, reading
outside under a tree in summer,
her dog at her side.

Just to tell you before things go bad,
this poem wants
to take a turn.
I want you to empathize and pat my back
when I tell you I've taken

care of my mother all my life.
I want you to feel sorry for me,
probably a lot, the way
I do for the adult ravens
suffering their ravenous twins.

See me hopping toward my mother.
There she is, her mouth open.
Waa!

Knock, Knock

The bad childhood joke is that everyone tells one.

The bad childhood joke is that your bad childhood is yours, the thing you clutch like the doll you clutched for three years and then lost, finding it one spring under a patch of overgrown weeds. You loved that doll, despite the bugs and weather that had eaten her hair, dug out her plastic eyes, torn her dress, lost her shoes. She was found! Oh, she was found, and then your father made you throw her away, your ruined baby, your love, all that feeling for three long years you'd whispered in her rubber ear, gone.

The bad childhood joke is that you pretend it doesn't exist, closing the door on its punch line, wham. Goodbye, stupid joke. But it knocks again. Who's there?

The bad childhood joke is that your childhood wasn't all bad. There are those summers at the pool, the girls you grew up with, swimming alongside them day after summer day, girls turned women you still lean close to and whisper with.

The bad childhood joke is death made it better.

The bad childhood joke was that even when it was better, the past hung in the house like your father's tobacco smoke. It cleared a little. You found you could breathe.

The bad childhood joke is three sisters walked into a bar. Only two walked out.

The bad childhood joke is that it wasn't your father's violent nature or strong hands that were the worst. It was your mother's nervous laughter.

The bad childhood joke is that you tried not to tell it to your children. You told another joke. Maybe not as bad. Maybe worse. You have heard them tell it a couple of times to girlfriends, almost laughing. You tried not to cover your ears.

The bad childhood joke is expensive. You pay for it for a long time.

The bad childhood joke is the joke that keeps giving even as you arc toward old age. It's the joke you tell best, perfecting each line down to the bone, your skeleton, the part of you made of light and air.

Dark Corners

The moon carried away the cat food, leaving her to turn over its absence. Was there extra? Would it last the long night? She checked the cupboards and counters

in the fake kitchen with the shallow metal sink and white microwave. Relief. There was plenty, but soon, with the cats eating all day from the always-filled

bowls, the kibble would disappear, as everything had. Look at her husband? Dead. Her youngest girl. Dead, too. Then where did her house go, sold to strangers. Stolen.

Her best furniture? Gone, put out on the sidewalk. Her favorite clothes weren't hung in her closet or folded in her dresser. Whose dresser was this? Where was her jewelry?

She walked the small rooms, searching for another bag of cat food. It hid in the memories she tried to catch in her hand. There, the story of her baby brother, born when she was twelve.

Why did anyone believe? Her mother too old for a baby! So they gave him to her, her baby, hers. They promised she could take care of him. Hers still, right?

He was hers, wasn't he, even after all that? It wasn't the neighbor's fault. Drunk when he arrived at her parents' party, famished, too busy to eat all day. In the back bedroom

the monster waited for her, hunched, dark, pressing her, pressing hard. She remembered that. When had she last seen the baby? Did he disappear when she went to college?

Was he still in her arms? At her stolen house? He never called. She didn't know where the cat food was. Her cats. Her babies. They would starve without her. That's what the moon did. They would all die. But everything died anyway. She must find the cat food. Where was it? Where was she? Who was hiding in the dark corners now?

Apology

I'm sorry I'm so slow,
not doing what I'm supposed
to, these things I'm paid for.

I'm sorry I can't drive.
Simply put, I shouldn't be on the road.
But here I am anyway.

I'm sorry I'm writing you a bad review.
I didn't read your book.
But it's what I think I'd feel.

I'm sorry I forgot to update the website,
refund your account, show up for the appointment.
It's been a hard week, you know?

I'm sorry that I'm late. That I don't have my paper.
That I'm not paying attention to anything you say.
I've got a life. I've got work. Shit happens.

I'm sorry for everything. For all of it.
For being too busy, too sad, too happy
to fulfill all your requests and fantasies.

To live the way you want me to,
you who know so much better, you,
sitting there right now,
you writing this.

Woman at Wash Basin

You can never undo the things
that you've done,
no matter the scalding water,
the stinging soap,
no matter the worry bead strands,
the loopy wooden rosaries you clutch,
matching your sins
to the saints you need the most.
No matter the daily flagellation,
the hairshirt,
the diets,
the marathons,
the long meetings,
the self-help books,
the ugly words
you say to yourself as
you walk your dog,
the exclamations
as you recall each wrong deed,
actions clacking
like dead marbles in your head,
if only your favorite tagline.

Easy to say
Don't do it.
But how to spot
the pleasant sentence
that train wrecks,
the causal remark
that ruins a life,
the unplanned slap
that ends it all,
the tease that leads
to a stumble off the cliff?

How to live in the time just after
the thing and before its result?

How to ride the wave
that never crashes into the
flat hard beach,
to stay standing through the earthquake
in its first giddy seconds
before the foundation crumbles,
to grab the roller coaster bar as it chugs
and lurches up,
never a down in sight?

Indiscrimination

She reads it *indiscrimination*,
and understands
how wantonness is systemic
but uncharted,
a fire we can't contain,
but one that dies
in an instant.

She has loved many
for few good reasons,
eaten the wrong calories
at the right times,
planted inappropriate
flowers in the freshly tilled
but frozen soil.

She's grown older,
but she's the girl
on the bridge,
answering the crucial question
in paragraphs
when a single word
would do.

It's her mantra, her *raison d'être*,
her cudgel, her wand,
her sword, her light.
It's her robe—a thousand
pounds heavy—her tilted
crown, her muddy ribbon hem,
her torn socks,
her lost shoes.

She's a scattered ant farm,
a dropped box of pins,
BB gunshot spilled on a wooden plank floor.

She's everywhere all at once,
looking behind herself
as she falls forward.

Separation

It's hard to be a
a whirling dervish
when you have to do the dishes,
when you have to keep on living.

In a swish of concise,
clean, poetic lines, I want to unfurl
the answer to my questions:

How long until I know what I'm here to find out?
How long can I manage to stay alone?

But I can barely swallow,
sadness stuck in my throat
like a bird
with one wing thrashing.

In the shower, I hold out my arms
and tell the universe I'm ready.

Silly me, I wait for an answer,
the water growing cold.

Outside the morning window,
birds. Deer. A fall sky
of radiant clouds.
An L of emerald lawn.
Live oak leaves.

Inside, everything else.

I Forget About Fame
– after Naomi Shihab Nye

The river is famous to the fish,
the way the sky is famous to an airplane,
the freeway famous to a car,
my house famous to me,
my office, desk, and chair,
mostly my chair, famous to my body,
mostly my ass.
My mother's reclining chair is famous
to her ass, as is my husband's work chair
famous to his rear.
Let's party! Bottoms up!

But wait. We're all sitting too much,
nothing to celebrate, and thus,
varicose veins are famous to our legs,
diabetes famous to all our organs,
heart disease famous to our circulatory systems,
obesity famous to our skeletons.
Imagine them, x-ray-wise, thin bones
pulling a rippled swell of hanging fatty folds,
a flap with each fleshy step.
What work! The skeletons should be famous,
but in this poem, they are not.

What should be famous is too time-consuming,
overwhelming, painful. Something to be forgotten,
avoided, so much easier to be bad,
to make famous the things that hurt us, like sugar,
which is famous to our adrenals.
Alcohol famous to our livers.
Drugs famous to our elaborate
edifices constructed of denial, fear, and apathy.

I don't want to be famous.
I don't want to be bad.

I want my skeleton to sit easy on my chair,
until it is time to pull my adequate proportion of fat
to the back yard.
I'm wearing sunscreen, so the sunlight is not famous
to my skin cancer, which I don't have.
Not in this revision.
No, I'm outside, breathing in the air
that is happily famous
to my clear lungs.
I walk the stone path,
on feet I can feel, touch
the mounded grasses
that are famous to the dirt,
and the dirt that is famous to them.

The wind blows through the elm.
I forget about fame.

Summer, 2020

The last dog walk
of the day is quick,
a fast pee before crating.

It is 9 pm, clouds
rosy as a blush,
Homer's dawny fingers,
but at night
and in a different sky.

Marcel is not interested
in sleep but in smells
on the neighbor's
emerald, immaculate
lawn, the rose bush
where he once dug
up a meaty steak bone
wobbly with age,
the clichéd yellow
fire hydrant on the corner
ringed with dead grass.

I wait, sigh, ignore
my impulse to yank
on the leash, eager
to be inside, to relax
in front of a mindless
movie that will peel
off the hard shell
of these weeks of fear
and dread and worry.

We pull past the California
poppies in their wrong
state, past the remains
of the bearded blue irises,
into the driveway

of the two elderly gay
men, who pretend
to be otherwise.

Instead of peeing,
Marcel curves into
pooping stance, me bereft
of bag, caught unaware,
again, my surprise
more embarrassment,
more shame. Inside the house,
the crackle of front window
shade, a V for viewing.

Barehanded, I scoop it up,
curling the brown
poo in my hand.
This a good one, solid,
warm, strangely
comforting. Marcel
wags his tail,
his eyes happy,
alert, and black.

Night is somewhere
at the edges.

Arrow/Bow

Arrow, shoots as straight as. Meaning, flies true.
Straight as an arrow, though, is an arrow straight?

Look that that triangle head, those wings, angles, surely,
straight ones. But arrows have geometric style.

Arrow, a weapon. Arrow,
a toy. Arrow, something from the Bronze Age,

though I'm making that up. Arrow from always.
Shooting an arrow, a skill we've forgotten, a skill

taught briefly in high school, round bullseyes
attached to hay bales, we with our gloves,

with our sleeves, a covering to protect
the softest skin. What, you might ask, were they thinking?

Thirteen-year-olds with arrows, with bows.
An arrow is nothing without a bow. Bow, a ribbon.

Bow, party dress. Bow, flowing. Said differently, bow, submissive.
Bow, adds aim. Bow brings weapon to target.

I have never been bow or arrow. Me, I'm the part in the middle,
the arrow released. The arrow quivering

but out of its quiver. Arrow arcing up, never
complete, arrow flying, flying home.

Benediction

May owls nest
in your attic,
a Sumerian curse
I cherish,
a call for a small,
wise creature on top
of things.
An owl awake,
watching,
a hunter, a provider,
head on a swivel,
wide-eyed and waiting.

The house, a ship.
The owl, the captain
gazing from the prow,
all of us moving forward
in the choppy
night, the owl
a guardian not a curse,
a salvation not a punishment.
May owls nest
in your attic.

Benediction.

The World Was Once an Ocean

I dabbled in ocean waters, nestled my body in the shallows, slid across its fine surface in boats.

But first, I crawled out, gasping, my flippers and fins and gills sodden. Then, at some point, I lurched across the plains to find myself in the middle of the middle. Hot earth in my clutched paws, palms.

Later, lots of walking on fours, on twos. Then boats. So many of them, from all directions. Then more dirt. More scrabbling. More yanking myself from place to place to finally land in this life exclusively on a coast that looks toward a sea I fly over.

No matter where I go, always, I come back to this western shore.

I am not sea-worn, bleached by water and salt and wind. I have no sea-legs, not even after a seven-day Baltic cruise. Not after rocking back and forth for hours on my grandfather's fishing boat. For hours after disembarking any vessel, I feel the water trying to pull me back.

I am a land person who can swim. A land person who loves the water. A land person wanting the interstitial, the intermediate, the place between the hot earth of the middle of middles and the depths of the far below.

I'm worn, cracked and brittle, dry to the touch. I'm a skein of dried kelp, sanded, airless, flattened. I'm driftwood pale, hollowed out from worries about mother, children, world.

The sea and I are old, distant friends. The sea ignores me, yet crashes at my feet, laps at my toes, throws forth mist and spray, insisting I remember the journeys.

I can take you back, the sea says. I can crush you, toss you high, rip away everything.

Don't take your eye off me.

Appreciation

I would first like to thank Hayley Haugen for appreciating my work and spending time on all these poems. It is a privilege to have them so guided into the world.

And thank you to all the editors who published some of these poems, provided editing notes, and awarded them prizes. You all helped me decide to start putting them together in a collection.

Thanks to folks in the writing round robin who read some of these, most especially Judy Myers who sets it up week after week and made thoughtful comments to a number of poems here.

My writing group—past and present members—commented on many of these poems. Thanks to Gail Offen-Brown, Ía Carbonell, Keri Dulaney-Gregor, Maureen O'Leary, Joan Kresich, Julie Roemer, and Judy Myers.

Maggie Smith, Traci Brimhall, and Kelli Agodon and the folks at Two Sylvias Press put on quite the poetry retreat in the summer, and a number of these poems were guided by the poets, the process, and the prompts. And thanks to Kris Whorton and Julie Roemer, both of whom have retreated with me these past two years and enriched theience.

To Kris Whorton, Julie Roemer, Warren Read, and Darien Gee. Thanks for reading the big bits and for providing the constant support: writing, moral, and spiritual. Thanks to Kari Flickinger, Darien Gee, and Traci Brimhall for reading and blurbing with such gracious words.

And I'm sorry if I've written about you. But I love you and must, though I made up a lot of stuff. Poetry is often fiction. My love and thanks to the following and prayers for forgiveness from those of you who can bestow it: Mitchell, Julien, and Jesse Inclán. Mitch, Carole, Sarah, and Rebecca Barksdale. Marcia Goodman. Kris Whorton. Jill and Ava Christofferson. Connie Hughes. Michael Rubin.

Sheila-Na-Gig Editions